GW00362945

contents

NZ, Canada, US and UK readers
Please note that Australian cup and spoon
measurements are metric. A quick conversion
guide appears on page 63.

chilli lime and chicken salad

1 cup (250ml) water
1 cup (250ml) chicken stock
340g chicken breast fillets
1 small carrot (70g)
1 small red capsicum (150g), sliced thinly
½ small chinese cabbage (200g), shredded finely
2 green onions, chopped finely
¾ cup (60g) bean sprouts
½ cup firmly packed fresh coriander leaves
100g watercress, trimmed
chilli lime dressing
¼ cup (60ml) lime juice
2 tablespoons sweet chilli sauce
1 clove garlic, crushed
1 tablespoon oyster sauce
1 teaspoon sesame oil

1 Bring the water and stock to a boil in medium saucepan. Reduce heat; add chicken, simmer about 10 minutes or until chicken is cooked through. Drain chicken; cool 5 minutes before slicing thinly.
2 Meanwhile, halve carrot crossways, cut each half into 2mm-wide lengths; cut lengths into matchstick-thin strips.
3 Place chicken and carrot in large bowl with capsicum, cabbage, onion, sprouts, coriander and watercress; add chilli lime dressing, toss to combine.
chilli lime dressing Combine ingredients in screw-top jar; shake well.

serves 4
per serving 4g fat (0.9g saturated); 669kJ (160 cal); 7.3g carb
on the table in 35 minutes

chicken and crunchy noodle salad

Crispy fried noodles are sold packaged (commonly a 100g packet) already deep-fried and ready to eat. They're sometimes labelled crunchy noodles and are available in two widths – thin and spaghetti-like, or wide and flat, like fettuccine.

4 chicken breast fillets (680g)
500g baby bok choy, shredded coarsely
250g cherry tomatoes, halved
50g fresh shiitake mushrooms, sliced thinly
¼ cup firmly packed fresh coriander leaves
1 cup (80g) bean sprouts
3 green onions, sliced thinly
100g crispy fried noodles
soy dressing
⅓ cup (80ml) light soy sauce
1 teaspoon sesame oil
2 tablespoons dry sherry

1 Cook chicken, in batches, on heated oiled grill plate (or grill or barbecue) until browned both sides and cooked through. Stand 5 minutes; slice thinly.
2 Meanwhile, make dressing. Combine bok choy, tomato, mushroom, coriander, sprouts and onion in large bowl.
3 Combine noodles with chicken, bok choy mixture and dressing; toss gently to combine.
soy dressing Combine ingredients in screw-top jar; shake well.

serves 4
per serving 7.6g fat (2.1g saturated); 1242kJ (297 cal); 10.6g carb
on the table in 20 minutes
tip The dressing should be added just before serving.

chicken tikka wrap

2 chicken breast fillets (340g)
1 tablespoon tikka masala curry paste
2½ cups (700g) low-fat yogurt
2 lebanese cucumbers (260g), seeded, chopped finely
⅓ cup coarsely chopped fresh mint
1 small red onion (100g), chopped finely
4 large pitta
100g mesclun

1 Cut each chicken fillet in half horizontally.
Combine chicken in large bowl with paste and
2 tablespoons of the yogurt.
2 Cook chicken, in batches, on heated lightly oiled
grill plate (or grill or barbecue) until browned all over and
cooked through. Stand 5 minutes; slice thinly.
3 Meanwhile, combine cucumber, mint, onion and
remaining yogurt in medium bowl.
4 Just before serving, spread yogurt mixture over
whole of each piece of bread; top with equal amounts
of mesclun then chicken. Roll to enclose filling.

serves 4
per serving 4.7g fat (0.9g saturated);
1150kJ (275 cal); 23.3g carb
on the table in 35 minutes

sticky barbecue wings

2 cups (400g) white long-grain rice
12 chicken wings (1kg)
¼ cup (60ml) barbecue sauce
¼ cup (60ml) plum sauce
1 tablespoon worcestershire sauce

1 Preheat oven to hot (220°C/200°C fan forced).
2 Cook rice in large saucepan of boiling water,
uncovered, until just tender; drain. Cover to keep warm.
3 Meanwhile, cut wing tips from chicken; cut wings
in half at joint.
4 Combine sauces in large bowl. Add chicken; toss
to coat chicken all over. Place chicken, in single layer,
in large oiled baking dish; roast, uncovered, about
20 minutes or until chicken is cooked through.
Serve chicken with rice.

serves 4
per serving 9g fat (2.8g saturated);
2671kJ (639 cal); 96g carb
on the table in 30 minutes

chicken with bok choy and flat mushrooms

2 tablespoons honey
⅓ cup (80ml) soy sauce
2 tablespoons dry sherry
1 teaspoon five-spice powder
4cm piece fresh ginger (20g), grated
1 tablespoon peanut oil
4 chicken breast fillets (680g)
4 flat mushrooms (360g)
500g baby bok choy, quartered lengthways
1 cup (250ml) chicken stock
2 teaspoons cornflour
2 tablespoons water

1 Combine honey, soy sauce, sherry, five-spice, ginger and oil in small jug. Place chicken in medium bowl with half of the honey mixture; toss to coat chicken in marinade. Cover; refrigerate 10 minutes.
2 Meanwhile, cook mushrooms and bok choy, in batches, on heated lightly oiled grill plate (or grill or barbecue) until just tender; cover to keep warm.
3 Cook drained chicken on same lightly oiled grill plate (or grill or barbecue) until browned both sides and cooked through. Cover; stand 5 minutes then slice thickly.
4 Meanwhile, combine remaining honey mixture in small saucepan with stock; bring to a boil. Stir in blended cornflour and water; cook, stirring, until sauce boils and thickens slightly.
5 Divide mushrooms and bok choy among serving plates; top with chicken, drizzle with sauce.

serves 4
per serving 9.3g fat (2g saturated); 1413kJ (338 cal); 16.2g carb
on the table in 35 minutes

chicken kebabs with papaya salsa

12 chicken tenderloins (900g)
1 small papaya (650g), peeled, seeded
4 green onions, sliced thinly
1 lebanese cucumber (130g), seeded, chopped coarsely
½ cup coarsely chopped fresh mint
2cm piece fresh ginger (10g), grated
1 tablespoon sweet chilli sauce
2 tablespoons lime juice

1 Thread chicken onto skewers. Cook skewers, in batches, on heated oiled grill plate (or grill or barbecue) until chicken is browned all over and cooked through.
2 Meanwhile, chop papaya finely. Place in small bowl with onion, cucumber, mint, ginger, sauce and juice; toss gently to combine. Serve kebabs topped with salsa.

serves 4
per serving 5.6g fat (1.4g saturated); 1258kJ (301 cal); 10.2g carb
on the table in 25 minutes
tips Soak 12 bamboo skewers in water for an hour before use, to prevent them from scorching and splintering.
You can substitute mango for the papaya if you prefer.

rosemary lamb open sandwich

4 lamb fillets (320g)
2 cloves garlic, crushed
¼ cup (60ml) lemon juice
2 tablespoons fresh rosemary leaves
1 tablespoon wholegrain mustard
2 small tomatoes (260g)
250g asparagus, halved
4 slices light rye bread
100g butter lettuce, chopped coarsely

1 Combine lamb, garlic, juice, rosemary and mustard in small bowl.
2 Cut each tomato into six wedges. Cook tomato and asparagus, in batches, on heated oiled grill plate (or grill or barbecue) until browned lightly and just tender. Toast bread both sides; keep warm.
3 Drain lamb; discard marinade. Cook lamb on same heated grill plate (or grill or barbecue) until browned and cooked as desired. Cover; stand 5 minutes before slicing thickly.
4 Place one slice of the toast on each serving plate; top each slice with equal amounts of lettuce, tomato, asparagus and lamb.

serves 4
per serving 8.1g fat (3.3g saturated);
941kJ (225 cal); 15.5g carb
on the table in 25 minutes
tip You can substitute toasted sourdough or ciabatta for the rye bread, if you prefer.

cajun lamb backstraps with four-bean salad

1 tablespoon cajun seasoning
800g lamb backstraps
1 small red onion (100g), chopped finely
2 small egg tomatoes (260g), chopped coarsely
60g baby spinach leaves, shredded finely
2 x 300g cans four-bean mix, rinsed, drained
¼ cup firmly packed fresh coriander leaves
¼ cup firmly packed fresh flat-leaf parsley
⅓ cup (80ml) bottled french dressing

1 Using hands, rub seasoning onto lamb; cook lamb on heated oiled grill plate (or grill or barbecue) until browned and cooked as desired. Cover; stand 5 minutes, slice thickly.
2 Meanwhile, place remaining ingredients in large bowl; toss gently to combine. Serve salad topped with lamb.

serves 4
per serving 12.5g fat (3.9g saturated); 1655kJ (396 cal); 19g carb
on the table in 25 minutes

korean-style barbecued cutlets

This recipe is an adaptation of the famous Korean barbecued dish bulgogi, where strips of beef are coated in a spicy mixture and barbecued over glowing coals. Today, a variety of meats – including chicken, pork and lamb – are cooked in this manner.

½ cup (125ml) light soy sauce
1 cup (250ml) mirin
2 green onions, sliced thinly
2 cloves garlic, crushed
4cm piece fresh ginger (20g), grated
1 tablespoon brown sugar
1 tablespoon cracked black pepper
1 tablespoon plain flour
16 lamb cutlets (1kg), trimmed

1 Combine sauce, mirin, onion, garlic, ginger, sugar, pepper and flour in large bowl. Add lamb, toss to coat all over with mixture; stand 10 minutes.
2 Cook drained lamb on heated oiled grill plate (or grill or barbecue) until browned both sides and cooked as desired. Brush occasionally with marinade during cooking. Serve with lime wedges, if desired.

serves 4
per serving 8.8g fat (3.9g saturated); 1141kJ (273 cal); 8.9g carb
on the table in 30 minutes
tip The cutlets can be marinated a day ahead and stored, covered, in the refrigerator.

lamb kofta with chilli tomato and yogurt sauces

1kg lean lamb mince
1 large brown onion
   (200g), chopped finely
1 clove garlic, crushed
1 tablespoon ground cumin
2 teaspoons ground
   turmeric
2 teaspoons ground
   allspice
1 tablespoon finely
   chopped fresh mint
2 tablespoons finely
   chopped fresh
   flat-leaf parsley
1 egg, beaten lightly
6 pocket pitta, quartered
yogurt sauce
200g low-fat yogurt
1 clove garlic, crushed
1 tablespoon finely
   chopped fresh
   flat-leaf parsley
chilli tomato sauce
¼ cup (60ml) tomato sauce
¼ cup (60ml) chilli sauce

1 Using hands, combine lamb, onion, garlic, spices, herbs and egg in large bowl; shape mixture into 18 balls.

2 Mould balls around skewers to form sausage shapes; cook, in batches, on heated oiled grill plate (or grill or barbecue) until browned all over and cooked through.

3 Serve kofta with pitta, yogurt sauce and chilli tomato sauce.

yogurt sauce Combine yogurt, garlic and parsley in small bowl.

chilli tomato sauce Combine sauces in small bowl.

serves 6
per serving 14.6g fat (5.8g saturated); 2136kJ (511 cal); 48.8g carb
on the table in 30 minutes
tip You need 18 bamboo skewers for this recipe. Soak them in water for an hour before use, to help prevent them from splintering or scorching.

beef donburi

Donburi refers to a certain size of rice bowl, usually with a lid, and also the meat or poultry/rice combination which is served in it. Koshihikari rice is grown from Japanese seed; substitute medium-grain white rice if desired.

1 cup (200g) koshihikari rice
500g beef rump steak, sliced thinly
1 clove garlic, crushed
1cm piece fresh ginger (5g), grated
½ cup (125ml) light soy sauce
½ cup (125ml) mirin
1 tablespoon peanut oil
6 green onions, sliced thinly

1 Cook rice in large saucepan of boiling water, uncovered, until just tender; drain.
2 Meanwhile, combine beef, garlic and ginger in medium bowl with half of the soy sauce and half of the mirin.
3 Heat oil in large frying pan; cook beef, in batches, stirring, until browned all over. Return beef to pan with remaining soy sauce and mirin; bring to a boil.
4 Serve beef mixture over rice; sprinkle with onion.

serves 4
per serving 13.2g fat (4.6g saturated); 1843kJ (441 cal); 42.1g carb
on the table in 25 minutes
tip You can use thinly sliced chicken breast fillets rather than beef in this recipe; if you do, thinly slice a large brown onion and add it to the chicken mixture before cooking.

beef and noodle salad

Bean thread noodles, also known as wun sen, glass or cellophane noodles, are made from mung beans. These delicate, fine noodles must be softened in boiling water before use; after soaking, they become transparent.

400g beef eye fillet steaks
2 tablespoons soy sauce
1 tablespoon sesame oil
250g bean thread noodles
1 medium red onion (170g), sliced thinly
1 large carrot (180g), sliced thinly
1 lebanese cucumber (130g), seeded, sliced thinly
½ cup loosely packed fresh coriander leaves
¼ cup coarsely chopped fresh thai basil
¼ cup (60ml) lime juice
¼ cup (60ml) sweet chilli sauce
2 tablespoons fish sauce

1 Combine beef, soy sauce and half of the oil in medium bowl; toss to coat beef in marinade.
2 Place noodles in large heatproof bowl, cover with boiling water, stand until just tender; drain. Rinse under cold water; drain.
3 Combine noodles in large bowl with onion, carrot, cucumber and herbs. Combine juice, sauces and remaining oil in small jug.
4 Drain beef; discard marinade. Cook beef on heated lightly oiled medium non-stick frying pan until browned both sides and cooked as desired. Cover; stand 10 minutes, then slice thinly. Add beef and dressing to salad; toss gently to combine. Serve with lime wedges, if desired.

serves 4
per serving 11.2g fat (3.2g saturated);
1250kJ (299 cal); 24.9g carb
on the table in 35 minutes

chilli pork noodles

Udon, wide Japanese noodles made from wheat flour,
are available fresh or dried from Asian supermarkets.
You can substitute any dried flat wheat noodle, but check
the manufacturer's instructions regarding their preparation.

500g udon
1 tablespoon peanut oil
2 tablespoons finely chopped garlic chives
3 cloves garlic, crushed
3 fresh small red thai chillies, seeded, chopped finely
500g lean pork mince
¼ cup (60ml) light soy sauce
½ cup (125ml) chicken stock
1 cup (80g) bean sprouts
4 green onions, sliced thinly

1 Cook noodles in large saucepan of boiling water,
uncovered, until just tender; drain.
2 Meanwhile, heat oil in wok; stir-fry chives, garlic
and chilli until fragrant.
3 Add pork; stir-fry until changed in colour and cooked
through. Add sauce and stock; stir-fry until hot. Serve
pork mixture on noodles; top with sprouts and onion.

serves 4
per serving 13.9g fat (4.2g saturated);
1614kJ (386 cal); 32.5g carb
on the table in 20 minutes
tip Dried udon are available in different thicknesses,
so the cooking time will vary depending on the size.

hokkien noodle and pork stir-fry

600g hokkien noodles
1 tablespoon cornflour
½ cup (125ml) water
¼ cup (60ml) kecap manis
¼ cup (60ml) hoisin sauce
2 tablespoons rice vinegar
2 tablespoons peanut oil
600g pork fillet, sliced thinly
1 medium brown onion (150g), sliced thickly
2 cloves garlic, crushed
1cm piece fresh ginger (5g), grated
150g sugar snap peas, trimmed
1 medium red capsicum (200g), sliced thinly
1 medium yellow capsicum (200g), sliced thinly
200g baby bok choy, quartered

1 Place noodles in large heatproof bowl, cover with boiling water. Separate noodles with fork; drain.
2 Blend cornflour with the water in small bowl; stir in sauces and vinegar.
3 Heat half of the oil in wok; stir-fry pork, in batches, until browned all over.
4 Heat remaining oil in wok; stir-fry onion, garlic and ginger until onion softens. Add peas, capsicums and bok choy; stir-fry until vegetables are just tender.
5 Return pork to wok with noodles and sauce mixture; stir-fry until sauce thickens slightly.

serves 4
per serving 14.3g fat (3g saturated);
2161kJ (517 cal); 52.4g carb
on the table in 30 minutes

sang choy bow

2 teaspoons sesame oil
500g lean pork mince
1 small brown onion (80g), chopped finely
1 clove garlic, crushed
1cm piece fresh ginger (5g), grated
2 tablespoons water
100g shiitake mushrooms, chopped finely
2 tablespoons soy sauce
2 tablespoons oyster sauce
1 tablespoon lime juice
2 cups (160g) bean sprouts
4 green onions, sliced thinly
¼ cup coarsely chopped fresh coriander
12 large butter lettuce leaves

1 Heat oil in wok; stir-fry pork, brown onion, garlic and ginger until pork is changed in colour and cooked through.
2 Add the water, mushrooms, sauces and juice; stir-fry until mushrooms are just tender. Remove from heat, add sprouts, green onion and coriander; toss gently to combine.
3 Divide lettuce leaves among serving plates; spoon pork mixture into leaves.

serves 4
per serving 11.4g fat (3.6g saturated); 1058kJ (253 cal); 8.1g carb
on the table in 30 minutes

pork and broccolini stir-fry

2 tablespoons peanut oil

450g pork steaks, sliced thinly

1 medium red onion (170g), sliced thinly

1 medium red capsicum (200g), sliced thinly

1 clove garlic, crushed

1cm piece fresh ginger (5g), grated

300g broccolini

1 teaspoon cornflour

2 tablespoons lemon juice

¼ cup (60ml) water

¼ cup (60ml) sweet chilli sauce

1 teaspoon fish sauce

1 tablespoon light soy sauce

1 teaspoon sesame oil

1 tablespoon coarsely chopped fresh coriander

1 tablespoon coarsely chopped fresh mint

1 Heat half of the peanut oil in wok; stir-fry pork, in batches, until browned.

2 Heat remaining peanut oil in wok; stir-fry onion, capsicum, garlic and ginger until vegetables are just tender.

3 Trim and halve broccolini. Blend cornflour with juice in small bowl; add the water, sauces and sesame oil. Stir mixture to combine.

4 Return pork to wok with broccolini and cornflour mixture; stir-fry about 2 minutes or until mixture boils and thickens slightly. Remove from heat; stir in coriander and mint just before serving. Serve with steamed rice, if desired.

serves 4
per serving 15g fat (3.4g saturated);
1225kJ (293 cal); 8.8g carb
on the table in 35 minutes

niçoise salad

100g green beans, trimmed
2 x 180g cans tuna in springwater, drained
1 small red onion (100g), sliced thinly
2 green onions, sliced thinly
250g cherry tomatoes, halved
100g mesclun
dressing
2 teaspoons finely grated lemon rind
½ cup (125ml) lemon juice
1 tablespoon wholegrain mustard
2 cloves garlic, crushed
2 teaspoons sugar

1 Boil, steam or microwave beans until just tender; rinse under cold water to cool. Cut beans in half.
2 Make dressing.
3 Combine beans with tuna, onions, tomato and mesclun in large bowl. Add dressing to salad; toss gently to combine.
dressing Whisk ingredients in small bowl.

serves 4
per serving 2.3g fat (0.8g saturated); 569kJ (136 cal); 7g carb
on the table in 20 minutes

oven-steamed ocean trout

4 x 200g ocean trout fillets
2 tablespoons lemon juice
1 tablespoon drained capers, chopped coarsely
2 teaspoons coarsely chopped fresh dill
1.2kg large new potatoes, sliced thickly

1 Preheat oven to moderately hot (200°C/180°C fan forced).
2 Place each fish fillet on a square piece of foil large enough to completely enclose fish; top each fillet with equal amounts of juice, capers and dill. Gather corners of foil squares together above fish, twist to close securely.
3 Place parcels on oven tray; cook about 15 minutes or until fish is cooked as desired. Unwrap and remove fish from foil before serving.
4 Meanwhile, boil, steam or microwave potato until tender. Serve fish with potato.

serves 4
per serving 7.9g fat (1.8g saturated); 1678kJ (400 cal); 35g carb
on the table in 25 minutes
tip Use tweezers to remove any bones from fish.

poached fish with herb salad

1.5 litres (6 cups) water
3 cloves garlic, crushed
6cm piece fresh ginger (30g), sliced thinly
8 fish fillets (880g)
2 limes, cut into wedges
herb salad
1 cup loosely packed fresh mint leaves
1 cup loosely packed fresh coriander leaves
1 cup loosely packed fresh basil leaves, torn
1 medium red onion (170g), sliced thinly
4 lebanese cucumbers (520g), seeded, sliced thinly
⅓ cup (80ml) fresh lime juice
4cm piece fresh ginger (20g), grated

1 Place the water, garlic and ginger in large frying pan;
bring to a boil. Add fish, reduce heat; simmer, uncovered,
about 5 minutes or until fish is cooked. Remove fish
with slotted spoon; discard liquid.
2 Meanwhile, make herb salad.
3 Serve fish with salad and lime wedges.
herb salad Combine ingredients in medium bowl.

serves 4
per serving 3g fat (1g saturated);
1124kJ (269 cal); 8.3g carb
on the table in 30 minutes
tip We used flathead fillets in this recipe.

grilled tuna with soba

Soba are Japanese buckwheat noodles similar in appearance to spaghetti. They are available dried from Asian food stores and some supermarkets.

4 tuna steaks (800g)
½ cup (125ml) mirin
2 teaspoons wasabi paste
½ cup (125ml) japanese soy sauce
1 sheet toasted seaweed (yaki-nori)
300g soba
6 green onions, sliced thinly
2 fresh long red chillies, chopped finely

1 Combine tuna with 2 tablespoons of the mirin, half of the wasabi and half of the soy sauce in large bowl; toss to coat tuna in marinade. Cover; refrigerate 10 minutes.
2 Meanwhile, using scissors, cut seaweed into four strips; cut each strip crossways into thin pieces.
3 Cook soba in large saucepan of boiling water, uncovered, until just tender; drain. Rinse under cold water; drain.
4 Meanwhile, cook tuna on heated lightly oiled grill plate (or grill or barbecue) until browned both sides and cooked as desired.
5 Combine soba in medium bowl with onion, chilli and combined remaining mirin, wasabi and sauce. Serve soba with tuna and seaweed.

serves 4
per serving 12.3g fat (4.8g saturated); 2475kJ (592 cal); 53.6g carb
on the table in 25 minutes

prawn tamarind stir-fry with bok choy

1kg uncooked medium king prawns
2 tablespoons peanut oil
4 green onions, sliced thinly lengthways
4 cloves garlic, sliced thinly
1 teaspoon cornflour
½ cup (125ml) vegetable stock
2 tablespoons oyster sauce
1 tablespoon tamarind concentrate
1 teaspoon sambal oelek
2 teaspoons sesame oil
1 tablespoon lime juice
1 tablespoon brown sugar
350g yellow patty-pan squash, sliced thickly
300g sugar snap peas, trimmed
800g baby bok choy, chopped coarsely

1 Shell and devein prawns, leaving tails intact.
2 Heat half of the peanut oil in wok; stir-fry onion and garlic,
separately, until browned lightly. Drain on absorbent paper.
3 Blend cornflour and stock in small jug; stir in sauce,
tamarind, sambal, sesame oil, juice and sugar.
4 Heat remaining peanut oil in wok; stir-fry prawns,
in batches, until changed in colour and almost cooked through.
Stir-fry squash until just tender. Add cornflour mixture; stir-fry
until sauce boils and thickens slightly.
5 Return prawns to wok with peas and bok choy; stir-fry
until bok choy just wilts and prawns are cooked through.
Serve stir-fry with steamed jasmine rice and topped with
reserved onion and garlic.

serves 4
per serving 13.2g fat (2.2g saturated);
1333kJ (319 cal); 16.4g carb
on the table in 35 minutes

stir-fried octopus with thai basil

1kg baby octopus
2 teaspoons peanut oil
2 teaspoons sesame oil
2 cloves garlic, crushed
2 fresh small red thai chillies, sliced thinly
2 large red capsicums (500g), sliced thinly
6 green onions, cut into 2cm lengths
¼ cup firmly packed fresh thai basil leaves
¼ cup (60ml) fish sauce
¼ cup (65g) grated palm sugar or brown sugar
1 tablespoon kecap manis

1 Remove and discard the head and beak of each octopus; cut each octopus in half. Rinse under cold water; drain.
2 Heat peanut oil in wok; stir-fry octopus, in batches, until browned all over and tender. Cover to keep warm.
3 Heat sesame oil in wok; stir-fry garlic, chilli and capsicum until capsicum is just tender. Return octopus to wok with remaining ingredients; stir-fry until basil leaves wilt and sugar dissolves.

serves 4
per serving 9.4g fat (1.8g saturated); 1877kJ (449 cal); 24.2g carb
on the table in 30 minutes

mussels with basil and lemon grass

1kg large black mussels
1 tablespoon peanut oil
1 medium brown onion (150g), chopped finely
2 cloves garlic, crushed
10cm stick fresh lemon grass (20g), sliced thinly
1 fresh small red thai chilli, chopped finely
1 cup (250ml) dry white wine
2 tablespoons lime juice
2 tablespoons fish sauce
½ cup loosely packed fresh thai basil leaves
½ cup (125ml) coconut milk
1 fresh small red thai chilli, extra, seeded, sliced thinly
2 green onions, sliced thinly

1 Scrub mussels under cold water; remove beards.
2 Heat oil in wok; stir-fry brown onion, garlic, lemon grass
and chopped chilli until onion softens and mixture is fragrant.
3 Add wine, juice and sauce; bring to a boil. Add
mussels; reduce heat, simmer, covered, about 5 minutes
or until mussels open (discard any that do not).
4 Meanwhile, shred half of the basil finely. Add shredded
basil and coconut milk to wok; stir-fry until heated through.
Place mussel mixture in serving bowl; sprinkle with sliced
chilli, green onion and remaining basil.

serves 4
per serving 12.1g fat (6.8g saturated);
869kJ (208 cal); 6.2g carb
on the table in 35 minutes

blue-eye cutlets with mango salsa

4 blue-eye cutlets (800g)

2 tablespoons lime juice

1 tablespoon fish sauce

1 tablespoon peanut oil

1 tablespoon grated palm sugar

1 teaspoon sambal oelek

2 kaffir lime leaves, shredded finely

mango salsa

2 large mangoes (1.2kg), chopped coarsely

2 lebanese cucumbers (260g), seeded, chopped coarsely

1 fresh long red chilli, seeded, sliced thinly

½ cup coarsely chopped fresh mint

1 Make mango salsa.

2 Cook fish, in batches, on heated oiled grill plate (or grill or barbecue) until browned both sides and cooked as desired.

3 Place remaining ingredients in screw-top jar; shake well. Divide salsa and fish among serving plates; drizzle with dressing.

mango salsa Place ingredients in medium bowl; toss gently to combine.

serves 4

per serving 6.3g fat (1g saturated); 1296kJ (310 cal); 31.9g carb

on the table in 35 minutes

roasted ratatouille with rye toast

4 baby eggplants (240g), chopped coarsely
3 small green zucchini (270g), chopped coarsely
100g button mushrooms, chopped coarsely
250g cherry tomatoes, halved
1 small leek (200g), chopped coarsely
2 cloves garlic, crushed
1 tablespoon olive oil
½ cup coarsely chopped fresh basil
1 tablespoon finely chopped fresh oregano
2 tablespoons balsamic vinegar
4 thick slices dark rye bread, toasted

1 Preheat oven to hot (220°C/200°C fan forced).
2 Combine eggplant, zucchini, mushrooms, tomato, leek, garlic and oil in large shallow baking dish; roast, uncovered, stirring occasionally, about 20 minutes or until vegetables are tender.
3 Stir basil, oregano and vinegar into ratatouille. Serve warm on rye bread.

serves 4
per serving 6.2g fat (0.8g saturated); 727kJ (174 cal); 22.2g carb
on the table in 35 minutes

singapore noodles

250g rice vermicelli
4 eggs, beaten lightly
2 teaspoons vegetable oil
1 medium brown onion (150g), chopped coarsely
2 cloves garlic, crushed
2cm piece fresh ginger (10g), grated
150g baby bok choy, chopped coarsely
200g snow peas, halved
1 small red capsicum (150g), sliced thickly
2 tablespoons soy sauce
2 tablespoons hoisin sauce
2 tablespoons sweet chilli sauce
1 cup loosely packed fresh coriander leaves
3 cups (240g) bean sprouts

1 Place noodles in large heatproof bowl, cover with boiling water, stand until just tender; drain. Using scissors, cut noodles into 10cm lengths.
2 Heat lightly oiled wok; add half of the egg, swirling wok to form thin omelette. Remove omelette from wok; roll into cigar shape, cut into thin slices. Repeat with remaining egg.
3 Heat oil in wok; stir-fry onion until soft. Add garlic and ginger; cook, stirring, 1 minute. Add bok choy, snow peas, capsicum and sauces; cook, stirring, until vegetables are just tender.
4 Add noodles and egg strips with coriander and sprouts to wok; toss gently to combine.

serves 4
per serving 9.1g fat (2g saturated); 1501kJ (359 cal); 51.9g carb
on the table in 30 minutes

mediterranean vegetables and haloumi bruschetta

1 small french breadstick
1 tablespoon olive oil
1 small eggplant (230g), sliced thinly
200g haloumi cheese, sliced thinly
2 tablespoons plain flour
2 medium egg tomatoes (150g), sliced thinly
2 tablespoons fresh baby basil leaves
1 tablespoon baby capers, rinsed, drained

1 Preheat oven to hot (220°C/200°C fan forced).
2 Cut bread, on an angle, into eight slices; brush both sides with half of the oil, place on oven tray. Toast, uncovered, in hot oven about 5 minutes.
3 Meanwhile, cook eggplant on heated oiled grill plate (or grill or barbecue) until just tender.
4 Coat haloumi in flour; cook on heated oiled grill plate (or grill or barbecue) until browned lightly.
5 Divide eggplant, haloumi, tomato, basil and capers evenly among bruschetta. Drizzle with remaining oil.

serves 4
per serving 14.6g fat (6.3g saturated); 1204kJ (288 cal); 24.2g carb
on the table in 25 minutes

eggplant, spinach and pumpkin stacks

1 large eggplant (500g)
coarse cooking salt
200g pumpkin, sliced thinly
700g bottled tomato pasta sauce
80g baby spinach leaves
4 green onions, sliced thinly lengthways
1 cup (100g) coarsely grated mozzarella cheese
¼ cup (40g) toasted pine nuts

1 Discard top and bottom of eggplant; cut eggplant lengthways into ten 5mm slices. Discard rounded-skin-side slices; place remaining eight slices in colander, sprinkle all over with salt; stand 10 minutes.
2 Rinse eggplant well under cold water; pat dry with absorbent paper. Cook eggplant and pumpkin, in batches, on heated oiled grill plate (or grill or barbecue) until tender.
3 Meanwhile, place sauce in medium saucepan; bring to a boil. Reduce heat; simmer, uncovered, 2 minutes.
4 Place four slices of the eggplant, in single layer, on oven tray; top with half of the spinach, half of the pumpkin and half of the onion. Spoon 2 tablespoons of the sauce over each then repeat layering process, using remaining spinach, pumpkin, onion and another 2 tablespoons of the sauce for each stack. Top stacks with remaining eggplant slices; pour over remaining sauce, sprinkle stacks with cheese and nuts. Place under hot grill until cheese browns lightly.

serves 4
per serving 13.3g fat (3.6g saturated);
1120kJ (268 cal); 23.4g carb
on the table in 35 minutes
tip Weight the eggplant when draining to extract as much water as possible; otherwise, the liquid causes the eggplant to soften and lose its shape when cooked. This process is called degorging.

mushroom, tomato and zucchini skewers with white bean puree

1 large red onion (300g)
200g button mushrooms
250g cherry tomatoes
2 large zucchini (300g), chopped coarsely
2 tablespoons balsamic vinegar
2 tablespoons olive oil
white bean puree
2 x 400g cans white beans, rinsed, drained
1 cup (250ml) vegetable stock
1 clove garlic, quartered
1 tablespoon lemon juice
1 tablespoon olive oil

1 Cut onion through the middle into 12 wedges.
2 Thread onion, mushrooms, tomatoes and zucchini equally among 12 skewers. Place skewers on large tray; drizzle with combined vinegar and oil.
3 Cook skewers on heated oiled grill plate (or grill or barbecue) until browned all over and tender.
4 Serve skewers on white bean puree.
white bean puree Combine beans and stock in large saucepan; bring to a boil. Reduce heat; simmer, uncovered, about 10 minutes or until liquid is absorbed. Blend or process bean mixture with garlic, juice and oil until smooth.

serves 4
per serving 14.7g fat (2.1g saturated); 1091kJ (261 cal); 21.2g carb
on the table in 30 minutes

glossary

allspice also known as pimento or jamaican pepper.

barbecue sauce a spicy, tomato-based sauce.

bean sprouts also known as bean shoots; new growths of assorted beans and seeds.

bok choy also known as bak choy, pak choi, chinese white cabbage or chinese chard; has a mild mustard taste; use stems and leaves. Baby bok choy (shanghai bok choy or pak kat farang) is smaller and more tender than bok choy.

broccolini a cross between broccoli and chinese kale. Each long stem is topped by a loose floret that resembles broccoli; from floret to stem, broccolini is edible whole.

cajun seasoning used to give an authentic spicy Cajun flavour to food, this packaged blend of assorted herbs and spices can include paprika, basil, onion, fennel, thyme, cayenne and tarragon.

capers grey-green buds of a warm-climate shrub, sold either dried and salted, or pickled; tiny capers, called baby capers, are also available.

capsicum also known as bell pepper or, simply, pepper. Discard membranes and seeds before use.

cheese

haloumi: firm, cream-coloured sheep-milk cheese matured in brine; can be grilled or fried, briefly, without breaking down.

mozzarella: soft, spun-curd cheese; originated in southern Italy where it is traditionally made from water buffalo milk.

chilli available in different types and sizes. Use gloves when seeding and chopping fresh chillies as they can burn skin. Removing membranes and seeds lessens the heat level.

small red thai: small, medium-hot and bright red in colour.

sweet chilli sauce: mild Thai sauce made from red chillies, sugar, garlic and vinegar.

chinese cabbage also known as peking or napa cabbage, wong bok or petsai; elongated with pale-green crinkly leaves.

coconut milk the diluted liquid from the second pressing of the white meat of a coconut (the first pressing produces coconut cream). Available in cans at supermarkets.

coriander also known as pak chee, cilantro or chinese parsley; leafy, bright-green herb with a pungent flavour.

cornflour also known as cornstarch.

cumin also known as zeera; available ground or as seeds.

eggplant also known as aubergine.

fish sauce also known as nam pla or nuoc nam; made from pulverised, salted, fermented fish (most often anchovies). Has a pungent smell and strong taste.

five-spice powder a fragrant mixture of ground cinnamon, cloves, star anise, Sichuan pepper and fennel seeds.

flour, plain an all-purpose flour, made from wheat.

garlic chives also known as chinese chives; strongly flavoured herb with flat leaves.

ginger also known as green or root ginger; the thick, gnarled root of a tropical plant.

hoisin sauce a thick paste made from salted, fermented soy beans, onions and garlic.

kaffir lime leaves look like two dark-green leaves joined end to end. Dried leaves are less potent so double the number if substituting them for fresh. A strip of fresh lime peel can be used in place of each leaf.

kecap manis thick, sweet soy sauce used in most South-East Asian cuisines.

lebanese cucumber small, slender and thin-skinned; also known as the european or burpless cucumber.

lemon grass sharp-edged, lemon-tasting grass; the white lower part of the stem is used.

mesclun salad mix of assorted young lettuce and other leaves, including baby spinach, mizuna and curly endive.

mince meat also known as ground meat, as in beef, pork, lamb and veal.

mirin a Japanese champagne-coloured cooking wine made of glutinous rice and alcohol; used expressly for cooking.

mushrooms

button: small, cultivated white mushrooms with mild flavour.

flat: large, flat mushrooms with a rich earthy flavour.

shiitake: also known, when fresh, as chinese black, forest or golden oak mushrooms. When dried, they are known as donko or dried chinese mushrooms; rehydrate before use.

mustard, wholegrain also
known as seeded; French-style
coarse-grain mustard made
from mustard seeds and
dijon-style french mustard.

noodles

bean thread: made from
extruded mung bean paste;
also known as cellophane or
glass noodles. Delicate and
fine; available dried in various-
size bundles. Soak to soften
before use; using them deep-
fried requires no pre-soaking.

crispy fried: crispy egg noodles
packaged already deep-fried.

hokkien noodles: also known
as stir-fry noodles; thick, yellow-
brown, fresh wheat noodles.

rice vermicelli: similar to bean
threads, but made with rice
flour. Soak before use (about
15 minutes), then boil briefly
and rinse with hot water.

soba: thin spaghetti-like pale-
brown noodle from Japan,
made from buckwheat.

udon: available fresh and dried,
these are broad, white, wheat
noodles, Japanese in origin.

onion

green: also known as scallion or
(incorrectly) shallot; onion picked
before bulb forms. Has a long,
bright-green edible stalk.

red: also known as spanish,
red spanish or bermuda onion;
sweet, large and purplish-red.

oyster sauce rich, brown
sauce made from oysters
and their brine.

papaya also known as
pawpaw; large, pear-shaped
red-orange tropical fruit.

parsley, flat-leaf also known
as continental or italian parsley.

patty-pan squash also known
as crookneck or custard
marrow pumpkins; a round,
slightly flat squash, yellow
to pale green in colour and
having a scalloped edge.

pine nuts also known
as pignoli.

pitta also known as lebanese
bread. This wheat-flour bread is
sold in large, flat pieces or small,
thick pieces (pocket pitta).

plum sauce thick, sweet and
sour sauce made from plums.

prawns also known as shrimp.

pumpkin also known
as squash.

rice

koshihikari: small, round-grain
white rice.

long-grain: elongated grain,
stays separate when cooked.

rice vinegar made from
fermented rice.

sambal oelek (also ulek or
olek); salty paste made from
ground chillies and vinegar.

sesame oil made from roasted,
crushed white sesame seeds;
used as a flavouring.

sherry fortified wine drunk as
an aperitif or used in cooking.

snow peas also known as
mange tout, or "eat all".

spinach also known as
english spinach and,
incorrectly, silverbeet.

stock 1 cup (250ml) stock is
equivalent to 1 cup (250ml)
water plus 1 stock cube (or
1 teaspoon stock powder).

sugar we used coarse table
sugar unless otherwise noted.

brown: soft, finely granulated
sugar retaining molasses for
its colour and flavour.

palm: also known as nam tan
pip, jaggery, or jawa or gula
melaka; usually sold in rock-
hard cakes; use brown sugar
if unavailable.

sugar snap peas also known
as honey snap peas; small
fresh pea eaten pod and all.

tamarind concentrate result
of distillation of tamarind juice;
ready-to-use product with no
soaking or straining required.

thai basil also known as
horapa; has smaller leaves
than common sweet basil,
as well as purplish stems
and a slight licorice taste.

tomato

bottled pasta sauce: prepared
sauce; buy at supermarkets.

cherry: also known as tiny tim
or tom thumb tomatoes;
small and round.

egg: also called plum or roma;
smallish and oval-shaped.

wasabi Japanese horseradish
traditionally served with raw
fish; sold as powder or paste.

white beans cooked white
beans are available canned;
varieties include cannellini,
butter and haricot beans. Any
can be used interchangeably.

wine we use good-quality
dry white and red wines.

worcestershire sauce a
thin, dark-brown spicy sauce
used as a seasoning for meat,
gravies and cocktails and
as a condiment.

yogurt, low-fat we used
yogurt with a fat content of
less than 0.2%.

zucchini also known as
courgette; belonging to the
squash family.

index

conversion chart

MEASURES

One Australian metric measuring cup holds approximately 250ml, one Australian metric tablespoon holds 20ml, one Australian metric teaspoon holds 5ml.

The difference between one country's measuring cups and another's is within a two- or three-teaspoon variance, and will not affect your cooking results. North America, New Zealand and the United Kingdom use a 15ml tablespoon.

All cup and spoon measurements are level. The most accurate way of measuring dry ingredients is to weigh them. When measuring liquids, use a clear glass or plastic jug with the metric markings.

We use large eggs with an average weight of 60g.

DRY MEASURES

METRIC	IMPERIAL
15g	½oz
30g	1oz
60g	2oz
90g	3oz
125g	4oz (¼lb)
155g	5oz
185g	6oz
220g	7oz
250g	8oz (½lb)
280g	9oz
315g	10oz
345g	11oz
375g	12oz (¾lb)
410g	13oz
440g	14oz
470g	15oz
500g	16oz (1lb)
750g	24oz (1½lb)
1kg	32oz (2lb)

LIQUID MEASURES

METRIC	IMPERIAL
30ml	1 fluid oz
60ml	2 fluid oz
100ml	3 fluid oz
125ml	4 fluid oz
150ml	5 fluid oz (¼ pint/1 gill)
190ml	6 fluid oz
250ml	8 fluid oz
300ml	10 fluid oz (½ pint)
500ml	16 fluid oz
600ml	20 fluid oz (1 pint)
1000ml (1 litre)	1¾ pints

LENGTH MEASURES

METRIC	IMPERIAL
3mm	⅛in
6mm	¼in
1cm	½in
2cm	¾in
2.5cm	1in
5cm	2in
6cm	2½in
8cm	3in
10cm	4in
13cm	5in
15cm	6in
18cm	7in
20cm	8in
23cm	9in
25cm	10in
28cm	11in
30cm	12in (1ft)

OVEN TEMPERATURES

These oven temperatures are only a guide for conventional ovens. For fan-forced ovens, check the manufacturer's manual.

	°C (CELSIUS)	°F (FAHRENHEIT)	GAS MARK
Very slow	120	250	½
Slow	150	275 – 300	1 – 2
Moderately slow	170	325	3
Moderate	180	350 – 375	4 – 5
Moderately hot	200	400	6
Hot	220	425 – 450	7 – 8
Very hot	240	475	9

Are you missing some of the world's favourite cookbooks

The Australian Women's Weekly cookbooks are available from bookshops, cookshops, supermarkets and other stores all over the world. You can also buy direct from the publisher, using the order form below.

MINI SERIES £2.50 190X138MM 64 PAGES

TITLE	QTY	TITLE	QTY	TITLE	QTY
4 Fast Ingredients		Curries		Party Food	
15-minute Feasts		Drinks		Pasta	
30-minute Meals		Fast Fish		Pickles and Chutneys	
50 Fast Chicken Fillets		Fast Food for Friends		Potatoes	
After-work Stir-fries		Fast Soup		Risotto	
Barbecue		Finger Food		Roast	
Barbecue Chicken		From the Shelf		Salads	
Barbecued Seafood		Gluten-free Cooking		Seafood	
Biscuits, Brownies & Biscotti		Ice-creams & Sorbets		Simple Slices	
Bites		Indian Cooking		Simply Seafood	
Bowl Food		Italian		Skinny Food	
Burgers, Rösti & Fritters		Jams & Jellies		Stir-fries	
Cafe Cakes		Kids Party Food		Summer Salads	
Cafe Food		Last-minute Meals		Tapas, Antipasto & Mezze	
Casseroles		Lebanese Cooking		Thai Cooking	
Char-grills & Barbecues		Malaysian Favourites		Thai Favourites	
Cheesecakes, Pavlovas & Trifles		Microwave		Vegetarian	
Chocolate		Mince		Vegetarian Stir-fries	
Chocolate Cakes		Muffins		Vegie Main Meals	
Christmas Cakes & Puddings		Noodles		Wok	
Cocktails		Outdoor Eating		TOTAL COST	£

Photocopy and complete coupon below

Name _____

Address _____

_____ Postcode _____

Country _____ Phone (business hours) _____

Email*(optional) _____
*By including your email address, you consent to receipt of any email regarding this magazine, and other emails which inform you of ACP's other publications, products, services and events, and to promote third party goods and services you may be interested in.

I enclose my cheque/money order for £ _____

or please charge £ _____ to my:

☐ Bankcard ☐ Mastercard ☐ Visa ☐ American Express ☐ Diners Club

Card number | | | | | | | | | | | | | | | | |

Cardholder's signature _____ Expiry date ____ /____

To order: Mail or fax – photocopy or complete the order form above, and send your credit card details or cheque payable to: Australian Consolidated Press (UK), Moulton Park Business Centre, Red House Road, Moulton Park, Northampton NN3 6AQ, phone (+44) (01) 604 497531, fax (+44) (01) 604 497533, email books@acpmedia.co.uk. Or order online at www.acpuk.com
Non-UK residents: We accept the credit cards listed on the coupon, or cheques, drafts or International Money Orders payable in sterling and drawn on a UK bank. Credit card charges are at the exchange rate current at the time of payment.
Postage and packing UK: Add £1.00 per order plus 25p per book.
Postage and packing overseas: Add £2.00 per order plus 50p per book.
Offer ends 30.06.2006